# SPIRITUAL NUGGETS

# SPIRITUAL NUGGETS
## A Devotional Book

*Ryburn T. Stancil*

*Exposition Press*    *Hicksville, New York*

*To*

*My Wife*

FANNIE MAE

# Preface

Many people who observe daily worship periods enjoy having a book of devotional readings to supplement their Bible reading and prayer. This book of *Spiritual Nuggets* was designed to meet that need. The Nuggets first appeared in the *Watauga Democrat,* a weekly newspaper in Boone, North Carolina, and in the *Terry Headlight,* a weekly newspaper in Terry, Mississippi. The response in both communities has been so encouraging that I thought a larger audience might be helped if a collection was published in book form.

Since the series has been running for several years, another volume will follow this one under the title *More Spiritual Nuggets,* if the reception of this volume justifies it.

My sincere thanks go to my wife, Fannie Mae, for reading the Nuggets and making many helpful suggestions.

Scriptures quoted are for the most part from the Revised Standard Version, though some are taken from the King James Version as indicated.

# Nugget One

*In returning and rest you shall be saved; in quietness and in trust shall be your strength.*

ISAIAH 30:15b

When the American scene was mostly rural, the people were generally God-fearing. Man lived close to nature, and he looked on nature as the work of God. There was no time clock to regulate his hours. He went to work with the rising sun, and closed his day when the sun went down. No boss determined his salary. Rather his income was regulated by the sun and the showers. His day began with a prayer for God's blessings, and ended on a note of gratitude to the God who had sustained him. He looked up into the starry heavens at night, and marvelled at the greatness of God. All of life for him was a cooperative enterprise between himself and God. Such was life when America was young!

To be religious was not difficult in those days. But the modern man rises to the blast of an alarm clock. He rides to work over paved highways in bumper-to-bumper traffic. He spends the day in an air-conditioned building with man-made gadgets and machines. Then when he has a day off his job, God's beautiful earth and starry heavens are all hidden from him behind a curtain of man-made smog. Everything he sees is the handiwork of man. There is so little to remind him of the reality of God. This modern man needs so much to be free from the rat race, that he may find fellowship with the eternal God.

Even in primitive times, in a rural society, a psalmist wrote, "Be still, and know that I am God" (Psalms 46:10). This writer felt the need for meditation in the presence of God. Jesus also once told his disciples, "When you pray, go into your room and shut the door and pray to your Father" (Matthew 6:6).

If such was necessary in those days, how much more do we

need today to find that separated place to meet with our God! If religion is to survive as a vital force, we must reserve some spot in our daily schedule for quietness and meditative prayer. We must separate ourselves from man's confusion, and expose ourselves to the stabilizing presence of God. God is still here and over the centuries he is saying to us, "Those that seek me diligently shall find me" (Proverbs 8:17b).

# Nugget Two

*So we know and believe the love God has for us. God is love, and he who abides in love abides in God, and God abides in him.*

I JOHN 4:16

The name of Judas Iscariot has borne its shame for many centuries because he betrayed one who had done him nothing but good. We often refer to such a person as the dog that bites the hand that feeds it.

But Judas should not bear this shame alone. Are not all of us guilty to a degree of this same ingratitude? Each time we sin, we are in rebellion against our greatest benefactor. Every hour of every day we are receiving expressions of God's love. James said it like this: "Every good endowment and every perfect gift is from above, coming from the Father of lights with whom there is no variation or shadow due to change" (James 1:17).

In these days of space travel, when we are beginning to know something of the barrenness and deadness of other heavenly bodies, we can better understand the wonder and beauty of our earth. God did something very special when he prepared this earth for us. Its air, its water, its life, its beauty—all these and more testify to God's love for us. He prepared a lovely dwelling place for man in the midst of a cold, dead universe.

His material benefits are not all in the past. He watches over us and sustains us every day. Each of life's daily benefits are but expressions of his boundless love.

His physical benefits, however, are but as nothing compared to that supreme sacrifice on our behalf when he gave his life on the cross for our redemption. The Apostle Paul wrote, "[God] made him [Jesus] to be sin who knew no sin, so that in him we might become the righteousness of God." (II Corinthians 5:21) On that cross Jesus made possible the salvation of all who would place their trust in him.

Is it not reasonable to say we share some of the guilt of Judas Iscariot when we sin against the God who loves us so, and who has blessed us in so many ways?

## *Nugget Three*

*Man is born to trouble as the sparks fly upward.*

JOB 5:7

*Blessed is the man who endures trial, for when he has stood the test he will receive the crown of life which God has promised to those who love him.*

JAMES 1:12

The hothouse plant withers quickly when exposed to chilling winds or unshielded sun. It lacks the toughness and enduring qualities of plants which have grown up in a natural environment.

The same is true of people who have been shielded from temptation and from the rougher experiences of life. Too much protection is poor equipment for facing the harsh realities of everyday living. Life is hard in spots, and when those trying days come we need a type of stamina that will stand up under most adverse conditions. This toughness grows out of enduring day by day trials along the way.

This is why James, the Lord's brother, wrote, "Count it all joy, my brethren, when you meet various trials, for you know that the testing of your faith produces steadfastness" (James 1:2-3). Paul once wrote, "We rejoice in our sufferings, knowing that suffering produces endurance, and endurance produces character" (Romans 5:3-4).

Certainly it is foolhardy to deliberately expose oneself or one's children to influences that might be destructive to morals or character. This is unnatural and unnecessary exposure, and could well lead to unhappy results.

But to try to live in, or to bring up children in an atmosphere that ignores the harsh realities of life, could result in such weak resistance to evil and to danger that they would become an easy target when unexpectedly exposed to temptation or to faulty teachings. Evil and pain and ugliness are all a very real part of our world—just as real as the good. It is a mistake to try to act or to bring up children as though these things do not exist. This type of isolation must sooner or later come to an end.

It is far better to recognize the reality of life's unpleasant side, and to train ourselves and our children to resist these things, and to overcome the evil with the good. Then when faced with unexpected testings we are not destroyed through weakness.

## Nugget Four

*For in him the whole fulness of deity dwells bodily, and you have come to fulness of life in him, who is the head of all rule and authority.*

COLOSSIANS 2:9-10

The ninth chapter of Luke's Gospel tells the story of the transfiguration of Jesus, when he appeared more a product of heaven than of earth. With him appeared the long-dead Moses and Elijah. Moses represented the Jewish Law. Elijah represented the Old Testament prophets. In the midst of this vision the apostles heard a voice coming out of the clouds proclaiming, "This is my Son, my chosen; listen to him" (Luke 9:35).

Devout Jews had always considered the Law and the Prophets as the final authority in matters of religious faith and practice. In the transfiguration God was designating Jesus as the new authority, replacing or supplementing both Moses and Elijah.

American culture has, over the years, recognized some rather rigid sources of authority. Social mores of the past, church pronouncements, Puritan ethics, and Biblical teachings have all combined to keep our culture in a fairly unyielding straightjacket.

A few years ago a rebellion set in against all recognized authority. In a relatively short time the whole American system of authority seemed to be crumbling. Freedom of expression, with no restraint, became our country's controlling passion.

Now, the evils growing out of unbridled freedom are becoming increasingly apparent. Ever larger numbers in every age bracket are recognizing that any society, to function with any satisfaction, must have somewhere a source of authority to which the will of the individual must bow. What we have not yet recognized is that we need to go back to that Mount of Transfiguration. We need to hear again the voice of God: "This is my Son, my chosen; listen to him."

Early gospel writers noted that Jesus spoke as one who had authority. He still does! We would all do well to make a fresh study of the life and teachings of Jesus. Obedience to him would solve America's problems, and give us the only real freedom man can enjoy. "Take my yoke upon you and learn of me, . . . and you will find rest for your souls" (Matthew 11:29).

# Nugget Five

*No one can serve two masters; for either he will hate the one and love the other, or he will be devoted to the one and despise the other. You cannot serve God and mammon.*

MATTHEW 6:24

History records many incidents of the American Indian trading things of real value for worthless trinkets, in their dealings with the white man. We often smile at their gullibility, and are amused at their sense of values. But do we have any room for amusement?

Have not many of us traded life's most valuable principles in exchange for the accumulation of dollars? Has not the financial affluence of recent years cost people spiritual values worth more than any bank account?

Jesus once said, "Take heed and beware of all covetousness: for a man's life does not consist in the abundance of his possessions" (Luke 12:15). Yet most of us are literally knocking ourselves out, trying to get as much of the world's goods as we can, believing this to be the true measure of success. Are we proving ourselves any wiser than were the savage Indians?

There is nothing evil about material wealth, but wealth is dangerous! Jesus said, "It is easier for a camel to go through the eye of a needle than for a rich man to enter the Kingdom of God" (Matthew 19:24).

Not many of us are spiritually strong enough to accumulate wealth without it becoming our first love, replacing God in our lives. Having the things we want is nice, but it's a poor bargain if it costs us our fellowship with God. "For what is a man profited if he shall gain the whole world, and lose his own soul?" (Matthew 16:26 KJV).

For the past few years our nation has experienced financial boom, bringing many needed benefits to our people. But it has also brought the risk that while our wealth accumulates, the spirit of our people might easily decay. To keep the proper balance, we need to redouble our efforts to strengthen our faith. Otherwise we may forget that it was God who gave us the natural resources and the wisdom to know how to turn those resources into a handsome profit. We must not twist our sense of values!

## *Nugget Six*

*For they loved the praise of men more than the praise of God.*
JOHN 12:43

Popularity is an intoxicating thing. Few people can endure constant praise and keep their heads. Once a person has tasted the goodwill of the masses, he finds it very difficult to do anything that will break that spell. Riding on the crest of public acclaim is so enjoyable and so exciting that most of us will compromise our convictions rather than offend our admirers. This is why Jesus said, "Woe to you, when all men speak well of you" (Luke 6:26).

If your ambition is personal promotion, you may be able to realize your goal for a while by agreeing with every person you meet, and doing all that they do in order to be sociable. This is the easy road, but the person who behaves this way makes no impact upon society for its improvement. At his death the world will be no better for his having lived.

To hold strong convictions, and to stick by those convictions, is not always the way to win friends, but it is the way to influence people. The person who really believes something, and sets out to right society's wrongs, will soon run into opposition. Some people will avoid him. Others will hate him. His popularity rating may reach a very low point. But his life will begin to have an impact. Others will be gradually persuaded to his position. Eventually the tide of public opinion will move in his direction. This type of man may die lonely and unappreciated, but he will have improved the quality of life for mankind, and monuments may be erected to his memory by future generations.

Each of us, to a greater or lesser degree, is choosing each day whether to do the popular thing in order to be accepted, or to do the right thing in order to improve the world. The latter course may earn us some enemies, but it will make our lives worthwhile, and will also gain the approval of God: and "if God be for us, who can be against us?" (Romans 8:31 KJV).

## *Nugget Seven*

*We know that we have passed out of death into life, because we love the brethren.*

I John 3:14

*Beloved, let us love one another; for love is of God, and he who loves is born of God and knows God. He who does not love does not know God; for God is love.*

I John 4:7-8

Christian love involves genuine goodwill toward the person loved. It crosses financial, social and racial barriers, and seeks the total welfare of every individual. Anything less than that falls short of New Testament requirements. This is the kind of love Jesus was talking about when he said, "You shall love your neighbor as yourself" (Matthew 22:39).

Few people find it difficult to love family, friend and benefactor. There is an element of selfishness in this, and human nature is selfish. But Christian love has no selfish overtones. It is self-giving without thought of personal gain. Concerning this Jesus said, "If you love those who love you, what credit is that to you? For even sinners love those who love them. And if you do good to those who do good to you, what credit is that to you? For even sinners do the same" (Luke 6:32-33).

The going gets tough though when we are instructed to "Love your enemies, do good to those who hate you, bless those who curse you, pray for those who abuse you" (Luke 6:27-28). This calls for something that is not a part of our natural equipment. Unredeemed humanity falters at this point. But this is what Jesus asks of his followers. This qualifies one to be called a child of God, because "he makes his sun to rise on the evil and on the good, and sends rain on the just and on the unjust" (Matthew 5:45).

This unselfish type of love is not something one can adopt at will. It is the product of the Spirit of God working in the heart of the person who is completely yielded to him. If you submit yourself to his lordship, he will give you a nature like unto his own. Then you, too, can love the unlovely and seek their welfare, no matter what they may do to you. This is love at its best. This is Christ-like love!

## *Nugget Eight*

*Judge not, that you be not judged. For with the judgment you pronounce you will be judged, and the measure you give will be the measure you get.*

MATTHEW 7:1-2

Most of us have telescopic vision when viewing the faults of our neighbors, but a blind spot when looking at our own. It's hard for us to see very much wrong with our behavior; but we quickly condemn every slip the other person makes.

We justify our own actions on the basis of circumstances, but give no such protection to others when they are at fault. "Why do you see the speck that is in your brother's eye, but do not notice the log that is in your own eye?" (Luke 6:41).

The whole problem grows out of man's unwillingness to admit or confess his sins, and to accept responsibility for them. Focusing attention on someone else's failures is just another device for diverting attention away from our own guilt.

This diversionary tactic is as old as the human race. Adam refused to accept his guilt, by blaming it on Eve. Eve disclaimed responsibility by saying it was the serpent's fault (Genesis 3:9-13). In the New Testament, when Jesus began to close in on the Samaritan woman's sin, she tried to lure him into a religious argument wherein she considered the Jews at fault (John 4:16-26).

The very first step in securing a healthy state of mind and a satisfying spiritual condition is to be honest with yourself, your neighbor and your Lord. If you are at fault, admit it! Don't try to cover up, or evade, or shift blame. You haven't been fooling anyone anyway.

Just accept yourself for what you are, and set out to make improvements, with God's help. This will leave you little room for being private sleuth on your neighbor's faults, or self-appointed judge of your fellowman.

## Nugget Nine

*Beloved, never avenge yourselves, but leave it to the wrath of God; for it is written, "Vengeance is mine, I will repay, says the Lord."*

ROMANS 12:19

Fighting back when you are mistreated is almost as natural as eating. The normal person's immediate reaction to wrong treatment is the urge to get even, or to repay the wrongdoer. After all, if you don't protect yourself and your rights, who will? This attitude grows out of the instinct of self-preservation.

Jesus vetoed this principle both in his life and in his teachings. When men cursed him, he never cursed back. When they struck him, there was no retaliation; and when they crucified him, he literally died praying for his persecutors.

All of this was in line with what he taught: "Ye have heard that it was said, 'An eye for an eye and a tooth for a tooth' but I say to you, Do not resist one who is evil. But if anyone strikes you on the right cheek, turn to him the other also; and if anyone would sue you and take your coat, let him have your cloak as well; and if anyone forces you to go one mile, go with him two miles" (Matthew 5:38-41).

The Apostle Paul echoed the same principle when he wrote, "See that none of you repays evil for evil, but always seek to do good to one another and to all" (I Thessalonians 5:15). And again, "If your enemy is hungry, feed him; if he is thirsty, give him drink; for by so doing you will heap burning coals upon his head. Do not be overcome by evil, but overcome evil with good" (Romans 12:20-21).

Hatred is never cured by responding with more hatred. It only aggravates the problem. Hatred can only be conquered by love. When an enemy is treated like an enemy, his enmity grows stronger. When he is treated as a friend, he is made ashamed. This is what Paul meant by "heaping burning coals upon his head."

Love may at first be ridiculed and spurned. But if love is genuine, it will eventually conquer far more effectively than retaliation. The goal of Christianity is not to win my rights, but to win my brother. This can be done only through love.

# Nugget Ten

*Rejoice in the Lord always; and again I say, Rejoice.*
PHILIPPIANS 4:4

When all the news media are blaring bad news around the clock, and an underlying pessimism pervades our whole society, it is startling to read the Biblical admonition, "Rejoice always" (I Thessalonians 5:16). What is there to rejoice about in a world such as ours?

To fully appreciate the force of this little two-word verse one needs to read II Corinthians 11:24-33. Paul is there cataloguing his hardships and persecutions. For a man with a history like that to write "Rejoice always" should make a modern pessimist ashamed of himself. If Paul could find reason for rejoicing, most of us should be able to. So again I raise the question, What is there to rejoice over in a world such as ours? There are many things. I mention only three.

At the head of the list is the fact that the eternal God loves us. There is no fact on which the Bible is clearer than this. His overall material provisions, his patience in dealing with our disobedience, and his provision for our eternal salvation all testify to his love. When we persist in being rebellious and going contrary to his will, he punishes, but it is always a redemptive punishment. "For the Lord disciplines him whom he loves, and chastises every son whom he receives" (Hebrews 12:6).

Another reason for rejoicing is that all power is in God's hands. He is able to do what he wills to do. Any limitation to his power is self-imposed. In granting man freedom God limits himself. But if man's freedom gets too far out of hand, then God's power is brought back into play for man's preservation. It is truly cause for rejoicing to know that a God with limitless power loves us with an everlasting love.

Then there is the biblical assurance that right and righteousness will eventually triumph over evil, no matter how things may look to the contrary. We are assured that evil will be destroyed and Christ and his followers will reign for ever and ever. The book of Revelation was written to give that assurance.

These are among the many reasons why Christians can smile through the tears of our times, and rejoice while the world is in the grip of despair.

# Nugget Eleven

*Then they cried to the Lord in their trouble, and he delivered them from their distress; he led them by a straight way, till they reached a city to dwell in.*

PSALMS 107:6-7

Why do God's children experience so many troubles and hardships? This question has puzzled good men of every age and generation. Certainly no adequate answer can be given in this short space. But here are a few suggestions.

In the first place, God does not spoil his children by showing them favoritism. They live in the same world and under the same natural laws as other people. They are subject to the same dangers in life as anyone else. If they get under a tree during a thunderstorm they are just as subject to be struck by lightning as anyone else under that same tree. Much of our suffering we bring on ourselves because we assume that God will give his children special protection from the natural laws of the universe. He doesn't, except on special occasions when they are preserved for a reason. Jesus said, "Thou shalt not tempt the Lord thy God" (Matthew 4:7 KJV).

Some suffering comes upon Christians because of the sins of other people. The drunken driver on the highway often brings tragedy and sorrow upon innocent people. Living in a world such as ours, we receive many unearned benefits from our fellowmen. It is also natural that we should also reap hurtful things from that same society, which we do not deserve.

The devil often brings sorrow, heartache and suffering upon Christian people in an effort to destroy their faith in the goodness and love of God. The story of Job in the Bible was written to illustrate that fact.

Of course some suffering comes from God's disciplinary actions. He punishes his children when they are disobedient. Like any good

23

parent, he doesn't overlook our misbehavior. He punished Adam and Eve. Many times he punished the Israelites as a nation. And he punishes his disobedient children today. "My son, do not regard lightly the discipline of the Lord, nor lose courage when you are punished by him. For the Lord disciplines him whom he loves, and chastises every son whom he receives. It is for discipline that you have to endure. God is treating you as sons: for what son is there whom his father does not discipline?" (Hebrews 12:5-7)

Whatever the source of your troubles, God can use them for your spiritual development, if you will take them to him in submission and faith.

# *Nugget Twelve*

*Ye are the salt of the earth; but if salt has lost its taste, how can its saltness be restored? It is no longer good for anything except to be thrown out and trodden under foot by men.*

MATTHEW 5:13

Rummaging through my desk a few days ago, I discovered a pack of red petunia seed. Looking at the picture on the packet I visualized the row of lovely petunias this packet of seed might have produced. But it didn't! The seeds were still safe in the desk drawer, dry and ungerminated. There in my hand I held uninvested life. Jesus said, "Truly, truly, I say unto you, unless a grain of wheat falls into the earth and dies, it remains alone; but if it dies, it bears fruit" (John 12:24).

A recent news item told of a man who died, leaving hundreds of thousands of dollars stuffed in bags in his apartment. This money proved worthless to him. It was wasted wealth because it was uninvested and unused wealth. It's hard for any of us to learn that what we keep, we lose.

The same principle holds with our Christian faith. A faith that is shared is a growing faith. But the faith we keep to ourselves gradually dries up and becomes ineffective even for ourselves. Church rolls are filled with members who entered the Christian fellowship with great joy and expectancy, but who now go through the routine motions of church attendance without any real meaning, or who no longer attend at all. They selfishly enjoyed their religion without sharing it with other people. Now it has atrophied, and they have lost their first love (Revelation 2:4).

"You are the light of the world," said Jesus. "Let your light so shine before men, that they may see your good works and give glory to your Father who is in heaven" (Matthew 5:14 and 16). Unshared Christianity is un-Christian. To bear its intended fruit in your own life, it must be planted in some other life. "Ye shall be witnesses unto me," said the Lord (Acts 1:8), and this is the road to a meaningful faith.

## *Nugget Thirteen*

*For in him the whole fulness of deity dwells bodily, and you have come to fulness of life in him, who is the head of all rule and authority.*

COLOSSIANS 2:9-10

In the springtime people often cut branches from fruit trees and place them in water to produce some early blossoms inside their homes. Such branches bloom beautifully, and add freshness to the atmosphere, but they produce no fruit. To be fruitful, they must remain attached to the parent tree. The same relationship exists between Christ and his followers. Jesus said, "As the branch cannot bear fruit by itself, unless it abides in the vine, neither can you, unless you abide in me. I am the vine. You are the branches. He who abides in me, and I in him, he it is who bears much fruit, for apart from me you can do nothing" (John 15:4-5).

Christianity is steadily losing ground in an increasingly pagan world, because of the failure to maintain a positive aggressiveness in world evangelization. There is little evidence of divine power at work in and through the churches. We formulate our plans, we make our decisions and we transact our business with a sort of hazy awareness that we are Christian. But to say we are operating under divine leadership, either in our individual or our corporate action, is often a drastic overstatement of the truth. More often we make our own decisions and pray the Lord to bless what we do. The results are evident.

Our connections with the Master are so loose, and so corroded with sin, selfishness and self-will, that any command he may issue to us, reaches us as a garbled staccato that we cannot decipher. We hear no clear voice of leadership from God, because we are actually not seeking his leadership. Like some cheap brand of produce that bears its maker's name only in fine print, we have a name that we are Christian, but for the most part are spiritually unattached.

A recognition of our own failures and our inadequacies, and a humble submission to his Lordship would renew the people of God as a conquering force in a sad and confused world.

## Nugget Fourteen

*If we say we have fellowship with him while we walk in darkness, we lie and do not live according to the truth.*

I John 1:6

*He who says he abides in him ought to walk in the same way in which he walked.*

I John 2:6

Most American adults are professing Christians. But what people are, and what they profess to be, are not always the same. Jesus said, "By their fruits ye shall know them" (Matthew 7:20).

One would like to think that all marital unfaithfulness, all dishonesty, all hatreds, all community friction and all degrading influences have their origin within the unchurched community; but we all know this isn't true. Even the prison population has a fairly high percentage of professing Christians.

Certainly none of us is perfect. But if we claim to be Christian, we should make a determined effort to keep our lives clean, and to live up to our profession. The Apostle John wrote, "By this we may be sure that we know him, if we keep his commandments" (I John 2:3). And again "By this it may be seen who are the children of God, and who are the children of the devil: whoever does not do right is not of God, nor he who does not love his brother" (I John 3:10). And Jesus said, "No good tree bears bad fruit" (Luke 6:43a). Jesus even challenges us to perfection: "You, therefore, must be perfect, as your heavenly Father is perfect" (Matthew 5:48).

To those who professed to be his followers the Master said, "Why do you call me Lord, and not do what I tell you?" (Luke 6:46). On another occasion he said, "Not everyone who says to me 'Lord, Lord' shall enter the kingdom of heaven, but he who does the will of my Father who is in heaven" (Matthew 7:21).

The lost world is hungry for a better way of life. Most of them realize the futility of their sinful ways. If they could see evidence in the church that Christ truly frees men from their sins, the churches couldn't seat the crowds that would flock into them. But the church's message is so diluted with its sinful behavior, that the world looks on in sad disillusionment. All our high-sounding proclamations have a terribly hollow ring when people observe our daily lives.

We hear much about the credibility gap in politics. There is often an even greater one in the Christian church. If the church is to be victorious in the world, it must first prove that it has won victory over its own sin.

# Nugget Fifteen

*Jesus said to them again, "Peace be with you. As the Father has sent me, even so I send you."*

JOHN 20:21

*For whoever is ashamed of me and of my words in this adulterous and sinful generation, of him will the Son of man also be ashamed, when he comes in the glory of his Father.*

MARK 8:38

Christians, as a rule, are strangely reluctant to talk about their religion. The greatest experience known to man is consistently given the silent treatment. People who are very vocal on other subjects, will clam up when religion is mentioned. Bruce Barton used to refer to this as the hush-hush that surrounds our faith.

Within itself, this behavior seems strange, but doubly strange when measured by New Testament practice. Jesus said, "Ye shall be my witnesses in Jerusalem and in all Judea and Samaria and to the end of the earth" (Acts 1:8b). In another place he said, "Ye are the light of the world. A city set on a hill cannot be hid. Nor do men light a lamp and put it under a bushel, but on a stand, and it gives light to all in the house. Let your light so shine before men, that they may see your good works and give glory to your Father who is in heaven" (Matthew 5:14-16).

The early Christians accepted this as their obligation and privilege. They even risked their lives, and some died, in order that men might know about Christ. Whatever their occupation, they became evangels of the faith. As a result, they literally turned the world upside down. They infiltrated every nation of the ancient world with the gospel of Christ.

You and I live in an age of intensified propaganda. Every facet of society uses personal salesmanship and mass media to make itself known to the public, and to proclaim its virtues. What a tribute to the vitality of Christianity that it survives at all in such a society, when it is so reluctant to make itself known!

One can't help but wonder what an impact the church would have on our world if its members caught the spirit of our times, and really set out to convince the world of the values and the joys of the Christian faith.

# Nugget Sixteen

*And my God will supply every need of yours according to his riches in glory in Christ Jesus.*

PHILIPPIANS 4:19

In the twelfth chapter of Luke's gospel, Jesus goes to some length to explain that God will provide for his own if they place his kingdom first in their lives and in their devotion. He urges them not to be anxious about life's necessities such as food and clothes, because the Father knows they need these things, and will therefore supply them.

He concluded the discussion by saying, "Do not seek what you are to eat and what you are to drink, nor be of anxious mind. For all the nations of the world seek these things; and your Father knows that you need them. Instead, seek his kingdom, and all these things shall be yours as well" (Luke 12:29-31).

Is Christ here commanding all his followers to resign their jobs and forsake all means of livelihood, and devote full time to kingdom service, depending upon God to supply their needs? Hardly! In Matthew's account paralleling this, it is more evident that the Lord is saying to put first things first. If the kingdom is our first concern, God will see that we do not suffer (Matthew 6:25-33).

Jesus cites, as proof of his argument, God's provision for the birds of the air and the lilies of the field. But this needs some explaining. God makes total provision for the lilies. Everything they need is supplied without any effort on their part. But the lily is not equipped to provide for itself. It is completely dependent, so God makes complete provision.

With birds we have a different story. God does not place food in their nest for them. He provides in nature the food they need and the materials to be used in making their nest. They have wings for flying, claws for scratching, and a bill with which to peck, if they make use of their native equipment. God makes available seeds and insects and other foods and building materials. The same principle applies in God's care of us.

The whole question is one of priorities. Christ wants his followers to gear all of life toward kingdom promotion. Whether at home, at work or at play, our kingdom responsibilities should shape our behavior. Our ultimate goal always and everywhere should be the glory of Christ and the advancement of his kingdom, rather than the fulfilling of personal plans and ambitions. So long as this is true God will bless our efforts in life, and we will never suffer want of the things we need.

## *Nugget Seventeen*

*A little one shall become a thousand, and a small one a strong nation.*

ISAIAH 60:22 KJV

*Are not five sparrows sold for two pennies? And not one of them is forgotten before God. Why, even the hairs of your head are all numbered.*

LUKE 12:6-7a

In a world fascinated with bigness, the importance of little things may easily be overlooked. Among the world's mighty nations no one was seriously interested in Hitler when he first started lecturing Germany's unemployed for the beginnings of Nazism. The world took no notice when the first little group of Russian Communists began meeting less than a century ago. Not very many people were impressed when Jesus gathered twelve working men about him for the first organized body of Christians.

These little things seemed insignificant when they were happening, but each was the beginning of a world-shaking movement. Jesus realized this in those early days when he said, "What is the Kingdom of God like? And to what shall I compare it? It is like a grain of mustard seed which a man took and sowed in his garden: and it grew and became a tree, and the birds of the air made their nests in its branches" (Luke 13:18-19).

What does all this say to us in these days of moon landings? Simply this: Any small service you perform for Christ could be the original seed of the most significant accomplishment of your life.

A mission Sunday School in a little mountain shack could be taking Christ to a boy who will someday shake the world with his preaching! A Christmas basket to a needy family may inspire a child in that home to later found a benevolent society to lift the lot of millions of the world's poor. A New Testament handed to a drunk person may be the turning point in a life that will later found an institution for the treatment of alcoholics. And so it goes.

If you can't do big things, do what you can! When dedicated to God, the little you can do may set up a chain reaction that will never end, and could conceivably change the course of history.

## *Nugget Eighteen*

*Now faith is the assurance of things hoped for, the conviction of things not seen.*

HEBREWS 11:1

In a materialistic age it isn't easy to accept spiritual things as real. We no longer doubt the possibility of the hydrogen bomb. This is something we can see and hear and feel. We are also convinced that man has been on the moon. We have seen him there! So we believe. But as to the reality of God and of the spiritual realm, many are in sincere doubt. "No one has ever seen God" (John 1:18). So, how do we know he is for real? Philip stirs the sympathy of many a modern man when he says to Jesus, "Lord, show us the Father, and we shall be satisfied" (John 14:8).

The truth is that God is as available to human experience as is the sunrise. But to experience the reality of God, one must first have faith that he is there. "Whoever would draw near to God must believe that he exists, and that he rewards those who seek him" (Hebrews 11:6).

Is this an unreasonable requirement? Certainly not! Every new scientific advancement is based on the same premise. No man ever heard the voice of radio until someone first believed it possible. No one ever saw a television screen until someone had first seen it by faith. No man ever stood on the face of the moon until there were those who had faith that it could be done. Before the goal could be reached, the journey had to be made in faith. Great truths of the spirit are the same. We must have faith in their reality before we can experience their truth.

God is very real to millions of people today around the world because they were willing to commit themselves unto him in faith. First they believed. Then they made a commitment on the basis of that faith. And God responded, and they *knew* that he was there. If you will genuinely trust him and commit yourself to him, you will know the truth and the truth will set you free (John 8:32).

# Nugget Nineteen

*Every plant which my heavenly Father has not planted will be rooted up. Let them alone; they are blind guides. And if a blind man leads a blind man, both will fall into a pit.*

MATTHEW 15:13-14

All people have problems. No person you meet on the street is without them. Most of us, sooner or later, need someone to help us with those problems. When we go in search of help, there are many sources available. Some are good and dependable. Some are not.

When seeking assistance one should be very careful whose advice or counsel he or she follows. "Blessed is the man who walketh not in the counsel of the ungodly" (Psalms 1:1a). A person who is not firmly grounded in faith in God is a poor source for guidance in any field of need. Unless he begins with God, he is a poor risk.

The physician who treats your body lacks the most important ingredient for healing if he fails to recognize the role God is playing in your recovery. When psychiatric help is needed, the first question the patient should ask is, "Are you a Christian?" If the answer is "No," the patient would do well to go elsewhere. The mind is man's most precious commodity. Any probing into its secrets should be done by a man of God. Otherwise the answers are bound to be wrong.

If the person who stands before you in a classroom is not a child of God, learn the facts he teaches, but be leery of his theories. No man without God is qualified to interpret truth. He can learn facts. He can impart those facts. But his interpretations begin from the wrong base. They are most likely to come out with the wrong conclusions.

Marital problems should never be taken to a counselor who is not devoutly religious. Marriage is life's most sacred relationship. It should not be entrusted to a person who does not know God.

"The fool hath said in his heart, There is no God" (Psalms 53:1). He is not the person I want to guide me in meeting life's problems!

## Nugget Twenty

*They received the word with all eagerness, examining the scriptures daily to see if these things were so.*

ACTS 17:11b

The vitality of the early Christian church was almost beyond belief. A small band of financially poor people, recruited mostly from the working class, literally shook the world's foundations in their time. This feat was accomplished in the face of violent persecutions. How could they do it?

Luke gives us a partial explanation: "They devoted themselves to the apostles' teaching and fellowship, to the breaking of bread and the prayers" (Acts 2:42). First of all, they were devoted to their task, and were well informed. There was a bond of fellowship among them, and they realized their dependence upon God. This is a good recipe for a dynamic church today.

The modern church has many members, lovely buildings and lots of money. But its members are only casually interested. There is a lack of wholehearted devotion. For those first-century Christians, God's work came first. This was their most important secret.

They devoted themselves to the apostles' teachings. They learned their doctrines, and so went out armed with knowledge. They knew what they believed, and their strong convictions were based upon reliable knowledge.

Fellowship was a major factor in that original group. Instead of being a diverse crowd who came together to worship God, and left without speaking to each other, they were united in a bond of love. They enjoyed being together. We are told they went from house to house breaking bread together.

They had received a worldwide commission, and knew they faced an impossible task. It was quite an accomplishment just to survive in such a hostile society. But they had been told to win that unfriendly world to Christ. This assignment had brought that little band of Christians to their knees in prayer. Here was the source of their unbelievable power. They stayed in touch with God. Thus he was able to work through them.

When your church and mine "devote themselves to the apostles' teachings and fellowship, to the breaking of bread and the prayers," things will happen here too!

# Nugget Twenty-one

*And there is salvation in no one else, for there is no other name under heaven given among men by which we must be saved.*

ACTS 4:12

We once lived in a cotton-mill town. The chief industry of the community was the manufacture of towels. They were name-brand towels, sold in America's most fashionable stores.

Every towel was carefully screened by experts, looking for the slightest flaw in material or workmanship. If any imperfections were discovered, the name label was clipped off before the towel was offered for sale. The company was extremely careful to protect the reputation of that brand-name.

Christians also bear a name which they should always protect with utmost care. The apostle Paul admonished the Philippian Christians to "let your manner of life be worthy of the Gospel of Christ" (Philippians 1:27). Concerning the name of Christ he wrote, "God has highly exalted him, and bestowed on him the name which is above every name, that at the name of Jesus every knee should bow, in heaven and on earth and under the earth, and every tongue should confess that Jesus Christ is Lord, to the glory of God, the Father" (Philippians 2:9-11). It is this name of Christ which we assume when we become Christians. We should strive always to bring only honor to that sacred name.

The day we walked down the church aisle and made our profession of faith in Christ, we received our brand-name, so to speak. We were given our label. From that day on we have borne the greatest name on earth or in heaven.

The non-church community knows the name we bear. They are watching our every act. Any misbehavior of ours is given far more publicity than any good we may do. Therefore, on the job, in

35

the marketplace, on the highways, in the social hall, in the home, on the golf course—always and everywhere we are either bringing honor to that name, or making the name a subject of ridicule.

If you bear the name Christian, thank God for it! Then do your best to make it an honored name in every circle of your influence.

## Nugget Twenty-two

*In thee, O Lord, do I take refuge; let me never be put to shame! In thy righteousness deliver me and rescue me; incline thy ear to me, and save me! Be thou to me a rock of refuge, a strong fortress, to save me, for thou art my rock and my fortress.*

PSALMS 71:1-3

Ancient writers were often expert at packing an unbelievable amount of truth into few words. A classic example is Psalms 46:1: "God is our refuge and strength, a very present help in trouble." Here God is pictured as a shelter of protection, a source of strength, and a reservoir of help in times of special need.

The Israelite nation in Old Testament days had cities of refuge in each geographic area of their country. These cities were designed for protection of persons whose life was unjustly threatened. If a person accidentally killed someone, for example, and the dead man's family sought vengeance, the fugitive could flee to a city of refuge, and he would be protected from harm. He could live there in safety. It was out of this background that the psalmist wrote, "God is our refuge."

Another psalmist echoed the same thought: "He shall cover thee with his feathers, and under his wings shalt thou trust: his truth shall be thy shield and buckler, thou shalt not be afraid for the terror by night; nor for the arrow that flieth by day; nor for the pestilence that walketh in darkness; nor for the destruction that wasteth at noonday" (Psalms 91:4-6 KJV).

But God is not just a protective umbrella. He is also a power-house of strength for his people. When our own resources are exhausted, he gives us that second wind that enables us to gain victories when all the odds seem against us. Another psalmist expressed it this way: "Blessed are the men whose strength is in thee . . . They go from strength to strength" (Psalms 84:5-7a). Isaiah wrote, "He gives power to the faint, and to him who has no might he increaseth strength" (Isaiah 40:29).

Finally, we are told, "God is a very present help in trouble." In grief, in temptation, in critical illness—whatever troubles we may face, there is no maze of red tape before we can get to him. He is always there. Like a mother, ever sensitive to her baby's cry, God's response is immediate when we call on him for help. Sometimes he lifts our burden completely. At other times he gives us the needed strength to carry it ourselves. He never lets us down.

## *Nugget Twenty-three*

*Say to all the congregation of the people of Israel, You shall be holy; for I the Lord your God am holy.*

LEVITICUS 19:2

The goal of Christian living is perfection. Jesus challenged his disciples to "be perfect, as your heavenly Father is perfect" (Matthew 5:48). No Christian should be satisfied with anything short of that challenge. Each of us should strive daily to measure up, thus staying on our tiptoes to the very end of life. This will keep us growing.

Late in his ministry the Apostle Paul wrote, "Not that I have already obtained this or am already perfect; but I press on to make it my own, because Christ Jesus has made me his own. Brethren, I do not consider that I have made it my own; but something I do, forgetting what lies behind and straining forward to what lies ahead, I press on toward the goal for the prize of the upward call of God in Christ Jesus" (Philippians 3:12-14).

If our relationship with Christ is to be meaningful, it must be a growing relationship. This means our goals must always be beyond our immediate reach. We must be ever straining our spiritual muscles toward a goal that is elusive enough to keep us climbing. That goal is perfection. It makes room for improvement for the most devout of Christians.

Jesus never intended that one of his followers should at any point relax his efforts for improvement and growth. No matter how great our spiritual attainments, or how much we might outstrip our associates, there is no spiritual plateau where we can relax and coast in satisfaction. That mountain peak of perfection always towers above us as a challenge to keep us growing in Christ-likeness.

Bodies grow old, and are forced to slow down, but the spirit of man is not subject to the aging process. "Though our outer nature is wasting away, our inner nature is being renewed every day" (II Corinthians 4:16). This is the way it should be, and this is the way it will be if we keep striving toward that perfection.

# *Nugget Twenty-four*

*And he sat down and called the twelve; and he said to them, "If any one would be first, he must be last of all and servant of all."*

MARK 9:35

When the mother of James and John asked Jesus to award top spots in his kingdom to her two sons (Matthew 20:20), she was being typically human. The animal nature in us makes us want to be the man on top. It is our usual practice to use all of our native ability to outstrip other people. In the classroom, on the athletic field, in the business world, and often even in the ministry, the picture is much the same. Everyone, more or less, is striving for the top rung on the ladder in his or her particular field.

Jesus taught a different way of life. "Whoever would be great among you must be your servant, and whoever would be first among you must be your slave: even as the Son of Man came not to be served, but to serve, and to give his life as a ransom for many" (Matthew 20:26-28).

Jesus was not discouraging ones striving for excellence in his field of endeavor. A Christian farmer should always seek to be the best farmer possible, not in order to choke out competition and thus enrich himself. Instead, his motive should be to help supply the needs of mankind in all the world, and to share his farming know-how with less efficient farmers so they can produce enough to sustain their own needs. His struggle for excellence should be for the purpose of helping other people in their needs.

In the spirit of Christ, the Christian physician should seek to be the best physician possible, not in order to increase his personal riches, but that he might do more toward relieving human suffering. He should also share his advanced skills with the profession in general, both at home and abroad. In this way he can improve the whole healing process for the good of all mankind. The same principle should govern all Christians in their work.

If each of us would struggle as hard for human betterment as we now struggle for personal advancement, the Christian ideal would become present reality. This is love in action, and love is what Christianity is all about.

# Nugget Twenty-five

*For the love of money is the root of all evils; it is through this craving that some have wandered away from the faith and pierced their hearts with many pangs.*

I TIMOTHY 6:10

We have all heard the expression "Money talks." The truth of this is evident everywhere. In business, in politics, in the courts and in every other area of human endeavor, the man with money has the advantage over the poor. His words bear more weight, his opinions are more influential, and his opposition to a matter is very difficult to override—even in the affairs of the church. He is valued more for what he has than for what he is.

This, of course, is not right, but we are all aware that it is regrettably true. The saddest fact is that this evil is often in evidence in the church.

James wrote, "My brethren, show no partiality as you hold the faith of our Lord Jesus Christ, the Lord of glory. For if a man with gold rings and in fine clothing comes into your assembly, and a poor man in shabby clothing also comes in, and you pay attention to the one who wears the fine clothing and say, 'Have a seat here, please,' while you say to the poor man, 'Stand there' or 'Sit at my feet,' have you not made distinctions among yourselves, and become judges of evil thoughts?" (James 2:1-4).

Is James writing about your church? Or do you give the same welcome to rich and poor alike? If both a wealthy family and a poor family moved into your church community, would both receive the same attention in trying to recruit them for membership? These are important questions that tell something of the genuineness of your Christianity.

God loves people, not for what they have, but for what they are, and for what they have the potential of being. If we are to act like children of God, we should remember that human souls are the goal of the church, and the human soul is of equal value whether in rags or in riches—whether in a clapboard shack or in a white-columned mansion. If money talks in your church, don't forget that it is strongly silent in the halls of heaven!

## *Nugget Twenty-six*

*Owe no one anything, except to love one another; for he who loves his neighbor has fulfilled the law.*

ROMANS 13:8

*Forsake me not when my strength is spent.*

PSALMS 71:9b

A young beauty queen was hospitalized. Well-wishers and admirers had banked her room with flowers until it looked like a florist shop. Into this flowery display walked the girl's pastor. Pausing in the doorway and surveying the room, he exclaimed, "My, my, what lovely flowers!" "Yes" she replied, "Lots of flowers and no people." And she began to weep.

This little scene illustrates a weakness in our affluent society. Having more money than time, we often send our money where our presence is needed far more. In an overcrowded world there are lonely people everywhere—people who hunger to know that someone loves them.

Whether it comes in the form of floral design or as welfare checks, money brings scant satisfaction to the heart that is longing for love. People need people. The psalmist wrote, "I look to the right and watch, but there is none who takes notice of me; no refuge remains to me, no man cares for me" (Psalms 142:4).

Much of the unrest that has plagued our world in recent years is the outburst of human hearts hungry for the recognition that only love can supply. Sending our cold cash in whatever form, be it groceries, flowers, or a ton of coal, leaves the recipient still hungry for our companionship and our love. People sometimes desperately need what we can send, but oftentimes they need us more. "If I give away all I have" wrote the apostle Paul, "and if I deliver my body to be burned, but have not love, I gain nothing" (I Corinthians 13:3)

Our money can be used to meet the physical needs of people, and this we must do. But man is spirit, and his soul yearns for love. He needs to know that he is important to other people. Only personal attention can prove to him that this is true.

## *Nugget Twenty-seven*

*He gives power to the faint, and to him who has no might he increases strength.*

ISAIAH 40:29

Several years ago something new was added to automobiles. It was known as the passing gear, but served many purposes other than passing. It was a reserve source of power which was always available when extra power was needed.

When driving is normal, a car functions adequately without using this gear at all. Many people drive for months without even being aware that their car has a passing gear. Then an emergency arises and additional power is needed to get out of a difficult situation. The driver steps down hard on the accelerator and automatically calls in this reserve of power. He surges ahead and meets whatever emergency confronted him.

Christian living is a lot like that. When life is normal and activities are routine, it is hard to realize the Christian possesses anything beyond what belongs to others. The non-Christian seems to have what he needs, and it's hard for him to see how being a Christian would be of value to him.

To the Christian it is always evident that Christ is a constant source of strength, but this becomes evident to the world in times

of crises. When the going gets tough the non-Christian is dependent upon his own resources. At such times he finds them inadequate.
So mental and moral breakdowns often result. He had battles to fight
beyond his ability. Failure resulted because he did not possess that
spiritual passing gear.

The Christian, however, has tapped a boundless source of extra
power in Christ. "They that wait for the Lord shall renew their
strength, they shall mount up with wings like eagles, they shall run
and not be weary, they shall walk and not faint" (Isaiah 40:31).
This is Isaiah's poetic way of saying that God's child has a reserve
source of strength for life's emergencies.

Eventually life here comes to an end. To walk into that vast
unknown alone is a fearful experience. Outside of Christ, this is
life's supreme tragedy. But "whoever calls on the name of the Lord
shall be saved" (Acts 2:21). Death for him is a victory because
he enters his eternal reward. Both here and hereafter, the grace of
God through Christ is adequate for whatever experience we face.
He is our day by day strength, and he is our passing gear.

## *Nugget Twenty-eight*

*Now when they saw the boldness of Peter and John, and per-
ceived that they were uneducated, common men, they won-
dered; and they recognized that they had been with Jesus.*
ACTS 4:13

The church of the late twentieth century is the object of very
vocal criticism, and oftentimes pure contempt. Many people, especially the intellectual communities, are turning their backs on the
church, and are looking elsewhere for a cause they believe to be
more worthwhile. This is not a new experience for the church. Its
history is strewn with the abuse of its detractors.

There was a time in the ministry of Jesus when the crowds left
him. Turning to his disciples he asked, "Will you also go away?"

To this Simon Peter answered, "Lord, to whom shall we go? You have the words of eternal life" (John 6:67-68).

Some years later the apostle Paul, a highly elucated man, took note of the fact that Christianity was not appealing to the upper brackets of the community. "Not many wise men after the flesh," he wrote, "not many mighty, not many noble, are called: but God hath chosen the foolish things of the world to confound the mighty" (I Corinthians 1:26-27 KJV).

Taking the long look at Christian history, one discovers that its periods of most severe criticism have been followed by great spiritual revivals. When people have forsaken the church with its simple message of redemption, they have discovered the way to be exceedingly dark outside, and have come back in repentance to inaugurate a wave of spiritual renewal.

If history repeats itself, these are encouraging days. "The fields are already white unto the harvest" (John 4:35). The confusion of our day gives mute evidence of what a nonchurchgoing society can be like.

The church with all its weaknesses is still the only institution which offers any real hope for a sin-burdened world. Being made up of people, it will always have its blind spots. But the church, and the church alone, has the words of eternal life.

## *Nugget Twenty-nine*

*If you continue in my word, you are my disciples, and you will know the truth, and the truth will make you free.*

JOHN 8:31b-32

*Truly, truly, I say unto you, everyone who commits sin is a slave to sin . . . So if the Son makes you free, you will be free indeed.*

JOHN 8:34 and 36

People place great emphasis upon their love for freedom, but few if any really want to be free. It's in man's very nature to seek a master whom he can serve. Every man has something outside himself that virtually controls his life. There is really not much meaning to life without it.

Some are mastered by drink, others by drugs, and still others by sex. These enslavements we recognize for what they are, and upright men seek to avoid such enslavements. People who submit are looked upon as weaklings. They are to be pitied, and treated as sick.

But aggressive, capable men, with strength of character and leadership ability become just as enslaved by the business or profession which is their means of livelihood. It disrupts their home-life. It alienates their family. It takes away their sleep. It drives them day and night as mercilessly as any ancient slave driver. They eventually are left without any time they can call their own. It all belongs to the monster they serve.

Then there is the fellow who gets the first taste of accumulated wealth. He likes the feeling of having a healthy bank account. He enjoys owning stocks and bonds. So he increases his holdings until they become an obsession with him. He begins to deny himself and his family many of the better things in order to accumulate wealth. Whatever spirit of benevolence he once had dries up. His money becomes his master, and his freedom is gone.

Man is made to be mastered. He was created to be the servant of God. But having these other masters makes impossible the mastery of God. Jesus said, "No servant can serve two masters; for either he will hate the one and love the other, or he will be devoted to one and despise the other. You cannot serve God and mammon" (Luke 18:13). As long as you have an earthly master, you cannot be a true servant of God through Christ.

Christ invites you to become his servant or slave. "Take my yoke upon you and learn of me; for I am gentle and lowly in heart, and you will find rest for your souls" (Matthew 11:29). Other masters enslave you. Serving Jesus sets you free!

# Nugget Thirty

*Let us consider how to stir up one another to love and good works, not neglecting to meet together, as is the habit of some, but encouraging one another.*

HEBREWS 10:24-25

The world outside the church, and the critics within the church, seem to think the church should be an organization of perfect people; and because it isn't, it is the object of unmerciful criticism. Such a judgment completely misses the mark as to the purpose of the church.

The church was never meant to be an exhibition hall of saintly people. It is rather a spiritual hospital for those who are aware of their need for healing. Jesus was once severely criticised for associating with society's sinful rabble. He was expected to confine himself to the holy elite of the religious community. To this Jesus responded, "Those who are well have no need of a physician, but those who are sick; I am not come to call the righteous, but sinners to repentance" (Luke 5:31-32).

Invitations to church often meet with the following response, "The church is a bunch of hypocrites. You have people up there who do things I would never dream of doing." Such a statement suggests that if you aren't living right, you should stay away from church. The very opposite is true. Of all the people who need the ministry of the church, the person enslaved by sin has the greatest need. It is a tribute to him when he comes to church, knowing he is probably being stared upon by many accusing eyes. It is an evidence that he is aware of his need, and has come in search of help where he feels help can be found. Jesus said, "Blessed are those who hunger and thirst after righteousness, for they shall be satisfied" (Matthew 5:6).

Certainly there will always be some who use the church for a shield to hide their nefarious behavior. But most of those who attend church are there because they know they are falling short of God's perfection, and they need strength and encouragement to be better persons. They believe the worship, fellowship and study offered there will add incentive to more righteous living. The church also offers them a channel through which they hope to have a part in ministering to the needs of other people around the world.

## *Nugget Thirty-one*

*Fear not, for I am with you.*

ISAIAH 43:5a

*Even though I walk through the valley of the shadow of death, I fear no evil; for thou art with me; thy rod and thy staff, they comfort me.*

PSALMS 23:4

The eye of the Lord is upon us, observing everything we think or say or do. "Nothing is covered up that will not be revealed, or hidden that will not be known" (Luke 12:2).

This fact has often been used as a sort of threat to keep misbehaving people in line; but there is a positive and reassuring side to the all-seeing eye of God. He is not a superspy who wiretaps the inner chambers of your heart. He is a loving Father who watches over his own. "Even the hairs of your head are numbered" (Matthew 10:30).

Nothing is more comforting to the child of God than the awareness that he is never beyond the reach and knowledge of his heavenly Father. When confronted with danger, he knows God is near; and in confident trust he can dismiss his fears.

In times of temptation the Christian feels the living presence of his Lord near at hand to give him the needed strength for the hour. He knows he needs extra strength beyond his own, and is assured that that strength is available, because "God is faithful, and he will not let you be tempted beyond your strength, but with the temptation will also provide the way of escape, that you may be able to endure it" (I Corinthians 10:13).

When difficult decisions must be made, and any choice we make looks of doubtful value, the Christian is assured of available counsel. "If any of you lacks wisdom, let him ask God who gives to all men generously and without reproaching, and it will be given him" (James 1:5).

To be sure, God does not assume all our burdens, but he is always there to step under the load when we reach our extremity. His presence is not that of a judge to be feared, but rather of a Father to be loved and obeyed.

If we are disobedient, he punishes, not in anger, but in love. "My son, do not regard lightly the discipline of the Lord, nor lose courage when you are punished by him. For the Lord disciplines him whom he loves, and chastises every son whom he receives" (Hebrews 12:5-6).

## *Nugget Thirty-two*

> *And he said to him, "You shall love the Lord your God with all your heart, and with all your soul, and with all your mind. This is the great and first commandment. And a second is like it, You shall love your neighbor as yourself. On these two commandments depend all the law and the prophets."*
>                                                          MATTHEW 22:37-40

Christianity is not a religion of laws and established rules of conduct. Rather it is a faith that is governed by eternal principles. Jesus did not give us laws to govern our behavior toward him and toward others. He gave us the principle of love. If our behavior is governed by love, we need no laws. That is what Paul meant when he wrote, "Love worketh no ill to his neighbor; therefore love is the fulfilling of the law" (Romans 13:10).

Most people prefer law. It gives them something definite by which to measure themselves. A middle-aged deacon once said to me, "I enjoy tithing. This is one thing I can know I am doing exactly right." A tithe is a tithe and there's really no room for argument. But to live justly requires interpretation. We have to decide what is the just thing to do in each situation. The Golden Rule has to be interpreted. It doesn't spell out the details, and we want our details spelled out. That's why we prefer definite laws.

This is what was wrong with the Pharisees. They knew the rules and they lived by them. But they didn't understand the principles upon which the rules were based.

Jesus wants people to have such basic principles of life that no rules or laws will be necessary. This is what he was getting at when he said, "Woe to you Pharisees! For you tithe mint and rue and every herb, and neglect justice and the love of God; these you ought to have done without neglecting the others" (Luke 11:42).

Love at times may seem more lenient than law, but on the whole it is far more demanding. Unscrupulous men can manipulate laws, but love has no loopholes. If you love God with your whole being, and love your fellowman as you love yourself, you will do nothing that will violate the laws of either God or man.

# *Nugget Thirty-three*

*This is the day which the Lord has made; let us rejoice and be glad in it.*

PSALMS 118:24

Life is not easy for anyone. From the small child, deeply disturbed over a broken toy, to the old man giving up a wife of half a century, trouble is the companion of man.

Life's burdens, however, are made unnecessarily heavy by anticipation and worry. No matter what burden you bear, you can endure it for one day. It is when we borrow troubles from coming days that life begins to crush us. Each day contains enough to occupy us for that day, without involving ourselves in what the future might hold. This is what Jesus was telling us when he said, "Therefore do not be anxious about tomorrow, for tomorrow will be anxious for itself. Let the day's own trouble be sufficient for the day" (Matthew 6:34). As long as we deal with life's problems one day at a time, they are never great enough to overwhelm us.

God does not give us today the strength we will need next week. He only supplies today what we need today. When tomorrow comes, if it does, he will make us adequate for whatever we have to face that day. In the Model Prayer Jesus did not instruct us to pray for future needs, but "Give us this day our daily bread" (Matthew 6:11).

We cannot live unmindful of the future. A certain amount of long-range planning is necessary; but burdening ourselves with anticipated troubles places needless strain on nerves that are already under pressure. If you live triumphantly this day, you will find that this within itself will reduce the burdens of tomorrow.

## *Nugget Thirty-four*

*Cast thy bread upon the waters, for you will find it after many days.*

ECCLESIASTES 11:1

"Do not be deceived; God is not mocked, for whatever a man sows, that he will also reap" (Galatians 6:7). This principle is as old as time, and is as reliable as the sunrise. Plant cucumber seed, and you will never gather canteloupes. The nature of the fruit is contained in the seed, and no amount of effort to the contrary can change that.

This principle is not confined to nature, because nature is but a shadow of the real world which is spiritual. Reaping what you sow is a dependable law of life. Devote all of your time and energy to material things and to physical pleasure, and you will never grow a great spirit. You need not hope to give your life in devotion to passing things and then reap eternal blessings. Life just doesn't work that way. If you want genuine happiness now, and assurance of even greater things beyond the reach of time, you must be sowing spiritual seed along the way. Its just that simple. "For he who sows to his own flesh will from the flesh reap corruption; but he who sows to the Spirit will from the Spirit reap eternal life" (Galatians 6:8).

How then does one sow to the Spirit? The first essential is the worship of God as revealed in Jesus Christ. Worship is the heart of any religion. We must worship God every day. There is no substitute for this. It is the bedrock on which any spiritual house must be built.

Then study the life and teachings of Jesus. Study them until you begin to absorb his nature and think his thoughts. Jesus is the revelation of God the Father. If you would please God, you must develop in Christ-likeness. He must become the Lord of your life.

These two things inevitably lead to the third step—the living of a life of unselfish service to God and to your fellowman. As you give of yourself, forgetful of your own interests and desires, the better you will understand these words of Jesus: "Truly, truly, I say to you, unless a grain of wheat falls into the earth and dies, it remains alone; but if it dies it bears much fruit. He who loves his life loses it, and he who hates his life in this world will keep it for eternal life" (John 12:24-25).

# Nugget Thirty-five

*A time to keep silence, and a time to speak.*

ECCLESIASTES 3:7b

"Even a fool who keeps silent is considered wise; when he closes his lips, he is deemed intelligent" (Proverbs 17:28). These words of the ancient Hebrew writer have been quoted for thousands of years to emphasize the wisdom of holding your tongue while other people are talking too much. But silence can be carried too far.

There are times when a Christian should speak out, though it may be much easier to keep silent. In the fourth chapter of the book of Acts the young Christian church was being persecuted relentlessly in an effort to stamp out the entire movement. The leaders of the church were jailed for their activities. When released, they were commanded to preach no more. Wisdom seemed to say, "Sit tight for a while until the storm subsides." But these men went back to the streets with their message, and their speaking won the day.

There are times when right-minded people can't afford to keep silent. When evil forces set out to undermine morals in society, keeping silent is sinful. Christians should always make their voices heard when righteousness is threatened. We should also speak when our speaking will bring about needed changes, even if our speaking makes us unpopular with the majority of the people.

Wicked men start promoting social evils when such is highly unpopular. With dogged determination they keep pushing until they drive their opposition to defeat. They endure social condemnation for a while because they believe it will eventually prove financially profitable for them.

Should the spiritually minded man's zeal for righteousness be less determined than the worldly man's zeal for sin? Should he protect his own immediate safety, rather than take the risk of aggressive action? Will he risk less for human good than the carnal man will risk for gold?

Our troubled world needs badly to hear loud and clear the voice of the church speaking for righteousness, truth, morality and spirituality. Strongly promoted good, will eventually conquer evil in any situation. This is the great need of our day.

## *Nugget Thirty-six*

*Who knows whether you have not come to the kingdom for such a time as this?*

ESTHER 4:14b

There is a fascinating fable in the Old Testament that reads like this: "The trees once went forth to anoint a king over them: and they said to the olive tree, 'Reign over us.' But the olive tree said to them, 'Shall I leave my fatness, by which gods and men are honored, and go to sway over the trees?' And the trees said to the fig tree, 'Come you, and reign over us.' But the fig tree said to them, 'Shall I leave my sweetness and my good fruit, and go to sway over the trees?' And the trees said to the vine, 'Come you, and reign over us.' But the vine said to them, 'Shall I leave my wine which cheers gods and men, and go to sway over the trees?' Then all the trees said to the bramble, 'Come you, and reign over us.' And the bramble said to the trees, 'If in good faith you are anointing me king over you, then come and take refuge in my shade; but if not, let fire come out of the bramble and devour the cedars of Lebanon" (Judges 9:8-15).

It is always true when the better institutions of society are too busy to sense the needs of the hour, society turns to evil forces for leadership. Then good men are not willing to enter politics, the people have no choice but to elect evil men. When energetic young people fail to find opportunities for self-expression in the home, the church or the school, they will naturally seek release in the disreputable ways of the world. When the good turns them down, the bramble is always out there waiting with open arms.

It is easy for good men and women to become so involved with matters of secondary importance that they do not have time for the more important. When this happens, the void is always filled by those who will sacrifice the good of society for their own enrichment.

## *Nugget Thirty-seven*

*My son, keep my words and treasure up my commandments with you; keep my commandments and live, keep my teachings as the apple of your eye; bind them on your fingers, write them on the tablet of your heart.*

PROVERBS 7:1-3

Many recent voices have been raised against "the establishment." People in strategic positions in education and in government are seeming to reject the authority of anything past or present. We appear to be in an era of experimentation, without accepting any past achievement as valid. We are told this is a bold new day. But really there is nothing new about it.

The ancient nation of Israel experienced such an era when there was no recognized authority. It was known as the period of the Judges. "In those days there was no king in Israel; every man did what was right in his own eyes" (Judges 17:6). This was the darkest, most confused period in the history of that nation. It must always be so when the wisdom of the past is ignored. When man's desire for freedom leads him to reject the accumulated wisdom of the ages, he pays dearly for every morsel of freedom he is privileged to taste. As he casts off the bondage of the past, he finds himself entangled in the bondage of his own personal limitations; and this is a much more limited confinement than the one he has rejected.

Our society of recent days has reverted from adulthood to adolescence. We are sure we know more than our parents so we reject their wisdom of long experience. This means that our society, like any adolescent, will pay a dreadful price in needless blunders and tragedies, most of which could have been avoided if we had been willing to listen.

The final word, of course, has not been spoken. Each generation has its own contribution to make. But the builders of the hundreth floor of a skyscraper must build on top of the other ninety-nine. Otherwise they will find themselves just building another first floor.

## *Nugget Thirty-eight*

*He also told this parable to some who trusted in themselves that they were righteous and despised others.*

LUKE 18:9

Most of us overrate ourselves. We minimize our faults, and magnify our virtues. Recognizing this human weakness, the apostle Paul wrote, "For by the grace given to me I bid every one among you not to think of himself more highly than he ought to think, but to think with sober judgment" (Romans 12:3a).

We are in a better position to know ourselves than anyone else could possibly be. But we either bask in the praise of those who admire and love us, and convince ourselves of their high judgment; or we defend ourselves against unfriendly critics until we are satisfied that their judgment is unfair. Very few of us are willing to make an honest appraisal.

If we are to eliminate our weaknesses, we must recognize that they exist, and work toward correcting them. We must also examine our overrated virtues. Our enjoyment of praise can blind us to the truth. Self-satisfaction is not likely to encourage improvement. If we consider ourselves good, it is not likely that we will try very hard to be better.

To the Christian, Jesus should be the norm. Figuratively speaking, we should stand ourselves up beside him and take our measurements there. He is perfect, and has challenged us to be the same (Matthew 5:48). Every child of God should make an honest and continued effort to reach that goal. When measured by that standard, most of the starch goes out of our ego.

Progress grows out of dissatisfaction with things as they are. Character development is no different. Life on earth is the opportunity God gives us to develop our best possible selves. Lets not end up at some halfway point because we think we have already arrived!

## *Nugget Thirty-nine*

*Behold, thou desirest truth in the inward being; therefore teach me wisdom in my secret heart. Purge me with hyssop, and I shall be clean; wash me, and I shall be whiter than snow.*

PSALMS 51:6-7

*Create in me a clean heart, O God, and put a new and right spirit within me.*

PSALMS 51:10

On a February afternoon I was approaching my car in a hospital parking lot on the top of the Blue Ridge Mountains, where winter winds blow almost constantly. On both sides of a nearby street I noticed trees still brown with last summer's leaves. The wind at the time was blowing a gale that almost took me off my feet. I thought back over the past months of winter winds, and marveled that those leaves had not been blown off. What unbelievable tenacity!

A few weeks later those same leaves were dropping rapidly even on days when there was no wind. As the spring sap rose in the trees, new life began pushing its way out into the twigs, and the old leaves were quietly pushed off from within. What the severe outer forces had been unable to accomplish, the quiet inner forces had managed without fanfare.

We have here a parable of man's experience with sin. When sin once gets a firm grip on a person's life, it holds on tenaciously. In a thousand ways he may try to throw it off, and a thousand times be defeated. Again and again he is convinced he has conquered, only to fail again and fall into deep remorse and depression. Eventually he realizes he is fighting a hopeless battle. Many people at this point give up and sink permanently into a life of sin.

The sinner's only hope lies in Christ Jesus. When a person opens his heart to Jesus, and trusts him to fight his battle for him, the Lord enters that person's heart and gives him or her a new nature. Out of this new self comes the needed strength that forces out the old sin, not necessarily in a spectacular experience, but like the sap in those trees, the new life eases out into every daily experience, giving the needed strength to withstand temptations.

If Christ is really given a chance in a life, he will bring about miraculous changes. Things which were once most attractive and appealing, will become repulsive. The old nature gives way to the new! "Therefore if any one is in Christ, he is a new creation; the old has passed away, behold, the new has come" (II Corinthians 5:17).

# Nugget Forty

*A little yeast leavens the whole lump.*

GALATIANS 5:9

People incline toward being many-sided creatures with compartmented lives. Especially is this true of the American man. He starts the day as a grumpy, half-asleep homebody. He then changes into a driving, determined, skillful motorist manipulating his car through early morning traffic. On the job he becomes a diplomat working for promotion, or a hard-hitting boss with an eye on production. On the golf course he is a genial companion, enjoying the game. At night he becomes a social lion—a man among the ladies. Then on Sunday morning he changes suits, assumes a special Sunday School smile, and joins the fellowship of the religious. Each area of his life has its own characteristics, separate and distinct from the others.

In at least one respect, this is out of tune with the will of God. God does not intend that man's religion should be a separate compartment of his life. Instead, it should permeate all else with which he has to do. Listen to the words of Jesus: "The Kingdom of Heaven is like unto leaven, which a woman took, and hid in three measures of meal, till the whole was leavened" (Matthew 13:33 KJV).

If Christianity is genuine, it can never be a different compartment of life. It must be the motivating force behind and within the Christian's every action, at home, on the street, at work, at play and in the church. He is first of all a Christian in every circumstance. This unavoidably shapes his attitudes and actions in everything he does. Anything less than this makes something of a mockery of his Sunday religion.

Jesus said the first and great commandment is this, "Thou shalt love the Lord thy God with all thy heart, and with all thy soul, and with all thy mind, and with all thy strength" (Mark 12:30 KJV). This doesn't leave much out. If a man is to be a child of God, it must be an all-consuming relationship.

# *Nugget Forty-one*

*For the days shall come upon you when your enemies will cast up a bank about you and surround you, and hem you in on every side, and dash you to the ground . . . because you did not know the time of your visitation.*

LUKE 19:43-44

Several years ago my wife and I drove to Greenville, North Carolina, to observe a total eclipse of the sun. This was one of those rare experiences that come once in a lifetime. There were people there from many nations of the world to watch this remarkable phenomenon. Yet, during the period of the totality, cars were still passing with their headlights on. Some of the people were not even bothering to stop and take a look. For a very few minutes the opportunity was there, and it would probably never return for those people driving by. Still they were carelessly passing it up.

How often all of us neglect life's spiritual opportunities with the same carelessness, or lack of appreciation. This was true while Jesus walked among men, and was not appreciated. It is still true with us today.

When Jesus was approaching the close of his ministry, and his enemies were marshalling all their forces for his destruction, he said to his disciples, "The light is with you for a little longer. Walk while you have the light, lest the darkness overtake you" (John 12:35a).

On another occasion the Lord told a story of some virgins who went forth to meet a bridegroom, but had not made proper preparation. When he arrived they were at the wrong place, so they lost their opportunity. Jesus closed the story by saying, "Watch therefore, for you know neither the day nor the hour" (Matthew 25:13).

At still another time Jesus said, "Let your loins be girded and your lamps burning, and be like men who are waiting for their Master to come home from the marriage feast, so they may open to him at once when he comes and knocks" (Luke 12:35-36).

These scriptures, along with others, emphasize the fleeting nature of spiritual opportunities. Who knows what privileges that are open to us today may be closed in days ahead? While we have the freedom to enjoy what the churches have to offer, may none of us pass up these sacred opportunities like the people who didn't bother to stop their cars to see a total eclipse.

# Nugget Forty-two

*The earth is the Lord's and the fulness thereof, the world and those who dwell therein.*

PSALM 24:1

Moon landings and space probes are making it rather clear that our earth is something very special in our universe, when compared with other heavenly bodies. It was made this way for the benefit of man. God loves man with an everlasting love, and he has shown that love in the wonder of our world.

It must have been the springtime when the Psalmist wrote, "The earth is full of the goodness of the Lord" (Psalms 33:5). With the memory of moon pictures in your mind, look out your window at the green hills or the lush valleys, the forested mountains or the sparkling waters of a fresh stream. Listen to the song of the birds, and the quiet chatter of the wild animals in the forest. Breathe the fresh air of the mountain heights. Inhale the sweet odors of myriad blossoms, and of the fresh plowed earth. Pause from your busy life and enjoy some of the blessings of earth. Remind yourself that all of this is the love of God at work for the good of man.

We can return some of that love by preserving what God has given us. We can keep our streams pure and fresh and free of trash. We can preserve the purity of the fresh morning air. We can band together to eliminate man-made eyesores from our landscape. We can take pride in this beautiful garden called earth. We can add to its beauty by planting flowers and trees, and keeping well-groomed lawns. All of this is a way of working hand-in-hand with God.

The earth *is* full of the goodness of God. Let's keep it that way, instead of filling it with the trash of man's inventions!

# Nugget Forty-three

*For those who live according to the flesh set their minds on the things of the flesh, but those who live according to the Spirit set their minds on the things of the Spirit. To set the mind on the flesh is death, but to set the mind on the Spirit is life and peace.*

ROMANS 8:5-6

If our country is to long survive, we must come back to the recognition of two fundamental truths. One is the word of Jesus to the Samaritan woman, "God is Spirit" (John 4:24). The other is found in the creation story in the book of Genesis, "So God created man in his own image, in the image of God created he him" (Genesis 1:27 KJV).

Man is essentially a spiritual being, made in the image of God. He dwells temporarily in a physical body which has animal tendencies. He is always in danger of magnifying the body at the expense of the spirit. When this happens, man, who was created to be God-like, becomes the most degraded of all God's creatures. That which has the highest potential for spiritual good, sinks to the very lowest level of sensual evil.

We have witnessed a growing trend in this direction as our wealth has increased and our faith diminished. As wealth expands, people magnify physical enjoyment. This can so easily drift into exaggerated sensual pleasures until it obscures man's spiritual nature. We can so easily drift from our divine likeness into a sensuous animal. This is a part of what Jesus meant when he said, "Truly, I say to you, it will be hard for a rich man to enter the Kingdom of heaven. Again I tell you, it is easier for a camel to go through the eye of a needle than for a rich man to enter the Kingdom of God" (Matthew 19:23-24).

In such a moral collapse man's civilization crumbles, and his national life gradually sinks into oblivion. This has happened so many times in world history that it seems incredible that a nation of our enlightenment would drift down that same road. Yet here we go! The danger signs are out everywhere! Man cannot survive very long as an animal. His hope for survival lies in the fact that he is a child of God. This is the way God planned it, and this is the only road that doesn't lead eventually to catastrophe.

## *Nugget Forty-four*

*Truly, truly, I say to you, he who believes has eternal life. I am the bread of life. Your fathers ate the manna in the wilderness, and they died. This is the bread which comes down from heaven, that a man may eat of it and not die. I am the living bread which came down from heaven; if anyone eats of this bread, he will live forever.*

JOHN 6:47-51a

It's always sad to watch people searching frantically for something that is readily available. This is the lot of so many in our confused world. All ages seem to be searching for life purpose and personal fulfillment. Yet most wind up in a state of frustration and disappointment.

Each generation has its own means of escape when they reach the end of life's blind alleys. Many youths have turned to pot, alcohol and sex. The older generation was a little more constructive, in that they buried themselves in productivity and the accumulation of wealth, but it was still an escape. None of these satisfy the deeper yearnings of the human heart. Only Christ can do that.

How very strange it is that we try so hard to find something that can be had for the asking. Jesus said, "Come to me all who labor and are heavy laden, and I will give you rest. Take my yoke upon you, and learn from me; for I am gentle and lowly in heart, and you will find rest for your souls" (Matthew 11:28-29).

To a Samaritan woman who had sought fulfillment in sex, Jesus said, "Everyone who drinks of this water will thirst again, but whoever drinks of the water that I shall give him will never thirst; the water that I shall give him will become in him a spring of water welling up to eternal life" (John 4:13-14).

All other trips a person may take in search of a more meaningful life lead only to greater hunger following each period of satisfaction. But the person who comes humbly to Jesus Christ, trusting him and completely surrendering to his lordship, finds that peace which every person wants. He also discovers a life purpose with eternal significance.

Many centuries ago Jesus said to the multitudes, "You refuse to come to me that you may have life" (John 5:40). Strangely enough, it is still true!

## *Nugget Forty-five*

> *Then the seventh angel blew his trumpet, and there were loud voices in heaven, saying, "The kingdom of the world has become the kingdom of our Lord and of his Christ, and he shall reign for ever and ever."*
>
> REVELATION 11:15

Jesus saturated his teachings with references to a society within society which he called the Kingdom of God. This kingdom's citizens were to be people who had experienced a rebirth—a spiritual birth. They were to be a people whose natures had been radically changed. This was to be accomplished through the work of God in each person's heart in response to his or her faith in Jesus Christ (John 3:1-8, 16).

These newborn kingdom citizens were to be characterized by love—love to God and love to men. People whose lives were thus controlled by love would have no need for laws, for no one would willfully harm the person he loved (Romans 13:8 and Galatians 5:14).

Jesus promised that, after his death, he would send his Holy Spirit to live among his kingdom citizens, and thus give direction to kingdom activities. The fruit of the Spirit in kingdom lives would be "love, joy, peace, patience, kindness, goodness, faithfulness, gentleness, self-control" (Galatians 5:22-23).

When a person first exercised faith in Christ, the kingdom would be established in his heart and life. Then would begin a process of penetration, like yeast in a barrel of meal, until his whole life would be brought under the control of Christ—his family life, business life, social life, political life, in fact all of his living (Matthew 13:33).

The faith of this individual would be contagious, and others would be drawn to Christ. Thus the society within society, which began small like a mustard seed, would eventually become a mighty organization of transformed men and women, who in turn would have a transforming influence on the world that contained them (Matthew 13:31-32).

This was the society that Jesus envisioned and offered to his disciples. The vision captured their imagination. They were so impressed that they staked their lives upon it. They gave everything they were and had to the bringing of this kingdom to full fruition. Their success was stupendous. The whole ancient world felt the impact of their testimony and their zeal.

The millions who today bear the name Christian need desperately to see the vision they saw, and to exercise the same faith and zeal that was theirs. This would give us a new world, transformed by the power of God working in human hearts.


# *Nugget Forty-six*

*Christ loved the church and gave himself up for her, that he might consecrate her, having cleansed her by the washing of water with the word, that the church might be presented before him in splendor, without spot or wrinkle or any such thing, that she might be holy and without blemish.*

EPHESIANS 5:25b-27

The primary function of the church is conversion and instruction of the people, and not social action. Though a certain amount of social work can be a worthy part of a church's ministry, that should never be permitted to sidetrack the church from the preaching-teaching ministry.

After his resurrection Jesus gave his church its commission. Matthew's version is the longest: "All authority in heaven and on earth has been given to me. Go therefore and make disciples of all nations, baptizing them in the name of the Father and of the Son and of the Holy Spirit, teaching them to observe all that I have commanded you; and lo, I am with you always, to the close of the age" (Matthew 28:18-20).

The primary ministry of the church is still to preach and teach the good news about Jesus Christ. Jesus founded the church, and this is what he told the church to do.

If the church does a good job of teaching and preaching, the people it wins and instructs will go out into society and live by the example Jesus set and by the principles he taught. They will live clean lives, minister to human need, improve the lot of the poor and practice justice in all human relationships. But the church as such will confine itself to the task of man's spiritual development.

Law schools do not operate courts of justice. They train lawyers to do that job. Medical schools, as a rule, are not primarily involved in the healing ministry. They train doctors to go out and heal. The church likewise is a teaching agency, and those it teaches go out in personal social ministries. An important part of the curriculum of the church is social concern and social action. If the church is to be Christian it must have a social awareness, and must so train its members. But for the church to allow itself to become deeply involved in meeting all the needs of the people, as a church, would cripple that church in its God-given ministry of preaching and teaching. The compassion of Jesus was so great that he could not turn his back in the presence of human misery. But he asked those whom he healed not to tell it. He understood that if he tried to meet all their needs, there would be no time left for teaching.

The church must remain the teaching institution where people are spiritually reborn, and are then developed into concerned individuals. These concerned people can then go out into society to live lives of compassionate ministry to the needs of men. Every great movement for social betterment has grown out of the teachings of the church, but few of those movements were launched by the church itself. It must always be so if the church is to remain true to its God-given ministry.

## *Nugget Forty-seven*

*The heavens are telling the glory of God; and the firmament proclaims his handiwork. Day to day pours forth speech, and night to night declares knowledge. There is no speech, nor are there words; their voice is not heard; yet their voice goes out through all the earth, and their words to the end of the world.*

PSALMS 19:1-4

A Galilean official came to Jesus one day asking the Lord to heal his afflicted son. Jesus responded, "Unless you see signs and wonders you will not believe" (John 4:48).

It has always been true that people have equated God with the mysterious and the unknown. Man expects God to prove himself by something spectacular or unusual. As scientific investigation has uncovered more and more of the secrets of the universe, God has been assigned an ever smaller role, because the realm of the unknown is continuously reduced.

This is an erroneous approach to any true understanding of God. Scientific discoveries have not eliminated God. They have only discovered how he works. In many instances man has been able to duplicate things God has been doing for centuries. When this happens, the unthinking lose faith in God. "If man ever goes into a lab and produces something that lives," said one college student, "I will no longer believe there is a God." This is foolish reasoning. If I study a Ford automobile until I can reproduce one myself, this doesn't prove that the Ford Motor Company never existed.

God is at work all around us every day in sunshine and showers, in the trees of the forests and in the flowers that grow in the window. He is in the song of the bird, and in the ripple of the mountain stream. He is seen in the movement of the stars, and in every heartbeat that drives the blood through your veins. Above all else, God is to be seen in the lives of those who love him and live by his teachings. God is not confined to the spectacular. He is in evidence everywhere, even in the smallest, most common things of earth.

## *Nugget Forty-eight*

*But Moses said to the Lord, "Oh, my Lord, I am not eloquent, either heretofore or since thou hast spoken to thy servant; but I am slow of speech and of tongue." Then the Lord said to him, "Who has made man's mouth? Who makes him dumb, or deaf, or seeing, or blind? Now therefore go, and I will be with your mouth and teach you what you shall speak."*
EXODUS 4:10-12

In an uninhabited area on the east side of the Sea of Galilee, Jesus was teaching a multitude of people. As the day wore on, the crowds grew tired and hungry. Turning to his disciples, Jesus asked, "How are we to buy bread, so that these people may eat?" In desperation the disciples sought ways to meet the emergency. Finally Andrew said, "There's a lad here who has five barley loaves and two fishes; but what are they among so many?" Whereupon Jesus took these few loaves and fishes and adequately fed more than five thousand people (John 6:4-13).

While this story is a demonstration of the miraculous powers of Jesus, it is more. In a most vivid fashion it tells us that nothing, however small it may be, is without value when placed in Jesus' hands.

One day a humble woman, poorest among the poor, came into the temple and made her offering. It was the smallest of offerings, worth only a fraction of our penny. Jesus took this woman, with her almost worthless gift, and gave the world a message that has challenged the Christian church to sacrificial giving for almost twenty centuries. That woman's gift, blessed by Jesus' approval, has probably given the Christian church more financial support than any other gift ever made (see Mark 12:41-44).

God is not dependent upon great things in order to accomplish his work. Not one of Jesus' twelve apostles was in a place of community leadership when Jesus selected them. But under the power of Christ and the Holy Spirit they literally turned the world upside down (Acts 17:16).

You may be limited in abilities, and possess few of the world's goods, but if you are completely committed to the Lord Jesus, and have put your all at his disposal, you may well be one of his most valued and most valuable servants. When the world passes you by, and reckons you to be of little worth, don't despair. God will give your life eternal significance if you yield yourself completely to him.

# *Nugget Forty-nine*

*Whoever exalts himself will be humbled, and whoever humbles himself will be exalted.*

MATTHEW 23:12

*He who is least among you all is the one who is great.*

LUKE 9:48b

Some of the truths Christ taught seem never to get through to us. We read them. We readily agree to the rightness of them. We even quote them and teach them; but we seem never to realize that they should apply to us in our daily activities. Such a truth is found in John 13:1-17. This is the story of Jesus washing the feet of his disciples. Here the Lord is performing the work of a servant or slave. Among other things, he was teaching his followers that high position does not disqualify one for lowly tasks. He was leveling out human inequalities.

If you ever get the feeling that certain jobs are beneath your dignity, take a fresh look at the Son of God on his knees with a pan of water, washing dirt off the feet of Judas Iscariot. Watch him again in the carpenter shop earning a living with his bare hands, for the support of his mother, brothers and sisters.

Several times in my ministry I have entered the church early on Sunday morning and found dirt or trash left by some Saturday night group that had been there after the Saturday cleaning had been done. The natural thing to do, of course, was get the broom and dust pan, and clean things up. Invariably, early comers who caught me so engaged, have said, "When did you get to be janitor?" as though this were something beneath the dignity of the pastor.

Collecting garbage is just as honorable as being president of a corporation, because it is just as important to the welfare of society. No Christian should ever look on honest toil as being beneath his dignity. We all need to take a fresh look at the words of Jesus, "Whoever would be great among you must be your servant, and whoever would be first among you must be your slave; even as the Son of man came not to be served but to serve, and to give his life as a ransom for many" (Matthew 20:26-28).

## *Nugget Fifty*

*But if any one has the world's goods and sees his brother in need, yet closes his heart against him, how does God's love abide in him?*

I JOHN 3:17

Jesus has a word for us affluent Americans. "And when they had eaten their fill, he told his disciples, 'Gather up the fragments left over, that nothing be lost'" (John 6:12). The occasion was the feeding of the five thousand, when everyone was well fed, and they had an abundance of food to spare.

There are pockets of poverty scattered throughout our country, but most of us Americans are troubled more by excess weight than by hunger. Because of our abundance we have become tragically wasteful—wasteful of our land, our forests, our wildlife, our petroleum, our metals, and even our natural beauty. Our garbage cans are stuffed with good food from our tables, while starvation is rampant in many parts of our world. As others starve, we are troubled over how to dispose of our waste!

The world was designed by an all-wise and loving God who planned it to provide for the total needs of mankind. There is enough here for us all if nothing is wasted. With modern methods of transportation and our knowledge and means of preservation, the world's goods could be distributed so that no man would suffer want. This is possible if the race of man had the will to do it. Some of our present luxury would be curtailed and some of our freedom limited. But if we love our fellowman as Christians ought, the sacrifice should be made.

It is much easier to be flagrantly wasteful than to be sacrificially helpful. So we are accustomed to taking the easier road for ourselves, and are little moved by the tragic needs of our fellowman.

Having more than we need does not justify wastefulness. There are others who need it now, and there are unborn millions who will be needing it in the years to come. We have a moral obligation to stop our waste and to share our excess with the needy peoples around us and to the ends of the world.

## *Nugget Fifty-one*

> And he said to them, "Thus it is written, that the Christ should suffer and on the third day rise from the dead, and that repentance and forgiveness of sins should be preached in his name to all nations, beginning from Jerusalem. You are witnesses of these things . . . but stay in the city, until you are clothed with power from on high."
>
> LUKE 24:46-49

When Judas Iscariot, one of the original twelve apostles, hanged himself in remorse after betraying Jesus, the other eleven thought he should be replaced, thus keeping the number twelve intact. So they made a mental study of the Christian group, and decided among themselves that only two of them qualified for the office, according to the standards they set up. They then prayed that God would show them which of these two he wanted. When they finally got around to praying about it, they hadn't left God much of a margin of choice (Acts 1:15-26).

Months later God selected his man for the place. In a dramatic move he placed his hand on Saul of Tarsus, and transformed him into Paul the Apostle. Here was a man the eleven would never have considered. He was the most powerful opponent of the Christian movement. Yet, God saw the potential in the man, and selected him for the evangelization of the ancient world (Acts 9:1-22).

We are still making the same mistake the eleven apostles made. We make up our minds as to what we want before we begin praying for God's leadership. Then we pray his blessings on our decision. We rule out many possibilities before we are willing to give God a voice in what is done.

Pulpit committees set out to find a pastor for their church. They hold a meeting and decide on what they want in a pastor; then ask God to help them find him. He must not be over fifty. He must be cautious on the race issue. He must have an attractive wife, who is a good housekeeper, and who is active in the total church life, etc., etc. Having decided on what they want, their prayers become fervent. Though it is God's church, they want what they want in a pastor, and they expect God to bow to their wishes.

We act as though we think God can't be trusted with decisions which we consider really important. We must get these things worked out before we turn things over to him. This makes our praying little more than a religious front without meaning. If God is not a safe guide from the start to the finish, then he is not God at all.

# Nugget Fifty-two

*And do not fear those who kill the body but cannot kill the soul; rather fear him who can destroy both soul and body in hell.*

MATTHEW 10:28

*It is a fearful thing to fall into the hands of the living God.*

HEBREWS 10:31

This is the age of the positive approach. Few people want to hear the negative. "Don't ever say 'No' to a child," they tell us. "You will hamper his initiative." Repentance is a forgotten word; we are supposed to think positively. Hellfire-and-damnation sermons are completely out of place in our time, you know. This is an enlightened age. Don't think negatively. Be positive!! The sin concept is an unenlightened idea. The person is sick. He needs treatment, not punishment. This is no day for condemning. Rather, people should be challenged. This is the trend of the modern mind.

We tend to forget that Jesus opened his ministry with the admonition to repent. He later said, "The world hates me because I testify of it that its works are evil" (John 7:7). The dramatic picture of a hell with fiery flames and agonizing thirst did not originate from the preaching of some backwoods preacher. The idea for such a hell comes from the sixteenth chapter of Luke's gospel, and the Lord Jesus is the speaker.

In our space here, it is not possible to list the scores of references Jesus made to sin, to judgment and to hell. Any careful reading of the four gospels will make it clear to the reader that the positive approach of Jesus is drawn against a negative background. Live righteously, because sin is destructive. Serve God, because the devil is your enemy. Strive for heaven, for hell is a place of horror. It is a message of contrasts. "Enter by the narrow gate," said Jesus, "for the gate is wide and the way is easy that leads to destruction,

and those who enter by it are many. For the gate is narrow and
the way is hard, that leads to life, and those who find it are few"
(Matthew 7:13-14). Be positive, yes, but don't ever forget there is
a negative, a dreadful negative!

## *Nugget Fifty-three*

*To the Jews I became as a Jew, in order to win Jews; to those
under the law I became as one under the law . . . that I might
win those under the law . . . To the weak I become weak, that
I might win the weak. I have become all things to all men,
that I might by all means save some.*

I CORINTHIANS 9:20-22

On the day of Pentecost the early Christians witnessed a spectacular in-gathering of new converts. In one day, we are told, there
were added to the church three thousand souls (Acts 2:41). The
apostle Peter is often credited with this remarkable accomplishment,
because he was preaching when it happened. But it wasn't his ser-
mon alone that moved the crowds. The rest of the Christian group
were mingling with the crowds, telling the gospel message to them
in their own language (Acts 2:6).

Preaching is a necessary part of any church endeavor, but not
necessarily the most important part. In any preaching service there
are people of very varied backgrounds. There are wealthy and poor,
old and young, educated and ignorant, rural and city as well as
other varieties. In such a situation it is next to impossible to clothe
the message in language that will have the needed impact on all
who are present.

For Christianity to really reach the people, it must be presented
on a person-to-person basis, in language the person can understand.
Farmers can dress the gospel in farming terminology in order to
reach farmers. Jesus did (Matthew 13:3-9). The athlete can reach
the athletic-minded in their own familiar language. A New Testa-

ment writer did (Hebrews 12:1-2). Fishermen can bear the message to men who fish in terms that have special meaning to them. Jesus also set the pattern here (Mark 1:17). Military men can witness in the language of their trade. The apostle Paul did (Ephesians 6:13-18). And so it goes. Every man can give a personal witness within his own group with greater effectiveness than is possible for anyone else.

If every week the laymen in the church were busy witnessing to the people where they live, where they work and where they play, there would be a new Pentecost in the church every Sunday!

## Nugget Fifty-four

*The hour is coming, indeed it has come, when you will be scattered, every man to his home, and will leave me alone; yet I am not alone, for the Father is with me.*

JOHN 16:32

*And he who sent me is with me; he has not left me alone, for I always do what is pleasing to him.*

JOHN 8:29

There is a loneliness to righteous living, but the rewards are eternal. Great crowds followed Jesus, but few, if any, felt really close to him. They stood in awe of him. They argued among themselves about him. They sought the benefits of his power. Very few genuinely loved him. Though he moved constantly among multitudes, he was seldom invited into their homes. We read that "they went each to his own house, but Jesus went to the Mount of Olives" (John 7:53-8:1). Jesus said concerning himself, "The Son of Man has nowhere to lay his head" (Matthew 8:20). When he was dying on the cross only a few wept. Even his disciples fled and left him alone.

Man is a social creature, and hungers for social acceptance. That is why every new fad gains such rapid acceptance. Everyone else is doing it. As it spreads, the nonparticipant begins to find himself alone; and most of us can't endure aloneness.

The same pattern holds in the area of moral behavior. God has given us enduring moral principles to live by, but most people do not live by them very strictly. Those who do, find themselves more and more alone in their position. They become socially unacceptable. They are a wet blanket on the existing order. Sometimes they stand completely alone. This social rejection is more than ordinary people can endure. Most buckle under the pressure. Only those of sterling character and unshakable faith are strong enough to stand alone in an unfriendly society.

Being truly Christian is an uphill business, and is usually a lonely business, but the rewards are worth all its costs. No social approval here can compare with the joy that will come when the judge of all men shall say, "Well done, thou good and faithful servant . . . Enter into the joy of thy Lord" (Matthew 25:21).

## *Nugget Fifty-five*

*And the Lord will guide you continually, and satisfy your desire with good things, and make your bones strong; and you shall be like a watered garden, like a spring of water, whose waters fail not.*

ISAIAH 58:11

All of us easily recognize the difference between a stagnant pool and a fresh mountain stream. The pool forms a scum. It produces mosquitoes. Its smell is offensive. Even cattle are reluctant to drink of it. But the mountain stream is alive and active. It sparkles with freshness. It attracts the thirsty. It is clean and wholesome, and the life it produces would grace any man's table. With this difference in mind, Jesus said, "He who believes in me . . . out of his heart shall flow rivers of living water" (John 7:38).

Whether it involves the world or the church, when people drift away from Christ, stagnation sets in. There are all kinds of unpleasant overtones, and whatever in life may be produced will be detrimental to the common good.

When Christ is in the human heart, that heart becomes creative for good. Out of it flow clean thoughts, deeds of kindness, and spiritual concern for lost men. The Christian heart is also productive of ideas for the relief of human suffering, and for the improvement of human society.

This difference is possible because when Christ knocks on the door of a human heart, and is admitted, he leaves the door of that heart open toward God. From that day on, that life becomes a channel through which God is active in human affairs. Just as the mountain stream is the outlet for a reservoir of life-giving freshness that seems inexhaustible, so it is that the Christian life is an earthly outlet for heaven's wealth. Here again, the life-giving resources seem to be inexhaustible.

# *Nugget Fifty-six*

*All scripture is inspired by God and is profitable for teaching, for reproof, for correction, and for training in righteousness, that the man of God may be complete, equipped for every good work.*

II TIMOTHY 3:16

Though the Bible remains the best seller among the world's books, many who possess copies are strangers within its pages. It's almost like a foreign language to them. They find it just about the dullest reading they ever tackled, and the most difficult to understand.

Other people literally dwell with this book. It is like a dear friend to them—a companion that sustains them in every crisis, and enriches them in their daily living. The covers of their Bibles are frayed, and the pages well-worn. Many of the passages are committed to memory, and the best loved verses freely quoted. Why this difference?

Jesus said, "He who is of God hears the words of God; the reason why you do not hear them is that you are not of God" (John 8:47). To understand spiritual truth, one must be spiritually minded. As a starting point, he must be born of God. This takes place when a person realizes his need for God, and puts his trust in Jesus Christ as his Lord and Savior. In response, Christ comes into his life and gives him a new nature, with spiritual understanding. This new experience in Christ gives a person hunger for a greater knowledge of God. Almost automatically he turns to the Scriptures for that spiritual enrichment. God responds to his searching by speaking to his heart through those scripture passages. This is a part of what Jesus meant when he said, "Blessed are those who hunger and thirst for righteousness, for they shall be satisfied" (Matthew 5:6).

The Bible is a treasure house for abundant living. But its treasures never become apparent until we have yielded ourselves and our wills to the lordship of Christ. After the new birth the Scriptures become food for spiritual growth—an inexhaustible spring, from which flow life-giving truths.

## *Nugget Fifty-seven*

*Let the word of Christ dwell in you richly, as you teach and admonish one another in all wisdom, and as you sing psalms and hymns and spiritual songs, with thankfulness in your hearts to God. And whatever you do, in word or deed, do everything in the name of the Lord Jesus, giving thanks to God the Father through him.*

COLOSSIANS 3:16-17

In the Genesis story of Adam and Eve, the serpent made the two of them believe they had more to gain by disobedience than by righteousness. He made great promises, but robbed them of paradise.

Whether you accept the story as history or not, the principle of the story is as valid as if it were written yesterday. The temptation to sin always makes us believe that the way of sin is the way to the most delightful living. In the end, however, sin robs us of the things we cherish most. In their stead comes guilt, heartache, disappointment, and an almost complete absence of true happiness. The road of sin leads eventually to a dismal end.

The way of righteousness, at first appearance, seems to offer little except restrictions, limitations and self-control. It seems to make mockery of Jesus' statement, "If the Son therefore shall make you free, you shall be free indeed" (John 8:36). But the more we submit ourselves to the mastery and control of the Spirit of Christ, the more we find of the things that make life worth living. There is release from tension. There is freedom from guilt. There is an abiding peace within the soul. There is a sense of spiritual well-being and joy. Everything in all the world about us takes on a new beauty, because we are seeing it with a new and deeper appreciation. We also discover a deeper experience of fellowship with other Christians. This new life in Christ makes life worth living. This is what Jesus was talking about when he said, "The thief comes only to steal and kill and destroy; I came that they may have life, and have it abundantly" (John 10:10).

## *Nugget Fifty-eight*

*And Peter opened his mouth and said, "Truly I perceive that God shows no partiality, but in every nation any one who fears him and does what is right is acceptable to him."*
                                                        ACTS 10:34-35

Complete impartiality is almost an unknown quality in human affairs. Either unfair advantage or discriminating disadvantage is allotted to certain people, though they have done nothing to deserve it. The child of the wealthy has an unfair advantage over the child of the poor. Racial heritage has much to do with opportunities socially, financially and politically. Sex also, in varying degrees, determines the rewards of society. Other examples of undeserved discrimination are not hard to find.

Man and God differ radically at this point. God's attitude is evidenced in the preaching of John the Baptist: "Bring forth therefore fruits worthy of repentance, and begin not to say within yourselves, 'We have Abraham to our father,' for I say unto you, that God is able of these stones to raise up children unto Abraham. And now also the ax is laid unto the root of the trees: every tree therefore which bringeth not forth good fruit is hewn down, and cast into the fire" (Luke 3:8-9a KJV).

God is not impressed with your ancestry, your race, or your wealth. "The Lord sees not as man sees; man looks on the outward appearance, but the Lord looks on the heart" (I Samuel 16:7b). When you stand before God you stand there as an individual, and you are judged and rewarded as an individual. "But everyone shall die for his own sin; each man who eats sour grapes, his teeth shall be set on edge" (Jeremiah 31:30). Whether you be king or pauper, whether you be black, white or red, whether you be man or woman, whether you live in a mansion or a ghetto, if you approach God in faith and in humble submission to his will, you will be accepted by a loving Father, and be dealt with as an obedient son.

If, on the other hand, you are rebellious in heart, and disobedient in behavior, and selfish in human relations, no amount of credentials nor of prestige and power will enable you to storm the gates of heaven. There are no favorites before the throne of God.

# Nugget Fifty-nine

*The cedars in the garden of God could not rival it, nor the fir trees equal its boughs; the plane trees were as nothing compared with its branches; no tree in the garden of God was like it in beauty. I made it beautiful in the mass of its branches, and all the trees of Eden envied it, that were in the garden of God.*

EZEKIEL 31:8-9

During the Great Depression, when millions were jobless and many were hungry, a wealthy Carolina family spent a million dollars developing a lovely garden for public enjoyment. Their critics were legion. How could they be so heartless as to spend money lavishly on flowers, when so many people were in dire need of food!

When the garden was finally in use, thousands of the poor wandered through those winding footpaths among roses, azaleas, tulips and myriad other varieties of blossoming plants and trees. Here were people who could afford no beauty where they lived. Accustomed to surroundings that destroyed man's better self, they were here finding some relief from their drab existence. This was something they could not buy for themselves, but something the soul of man needed.

Watching this procession, one was reminded that Jesus once said, "Man shall not live by bread alone" (Matthew 4:4). Bread is essential, yes! But man is made in the image of God. He is not just animal. A vital part of his nature dries up without beauty. God recognized this need of man when he built the majestic hills, when he painted the western sunset, when he created the world of flowers, and when he gave us autumn colors and the silver-coated mountains in winter.

Our industrial giant of a nation is filling her coffers with gold, but destroying her beauty with pollution. We need fewer gadgets and more gardens, and some free time to enjoy them.

We are rightly concerned about the world's hungry mouths, but there is a deeper need that bread can never satisfy. Man also hungers for beauty, love and God. Without these, he must always be something less than man. Without these he will always be searching, in the midst of his apparent plenty.

## *Nugget Sixty*

*Peter said to him, "Even though they all fall away, I will not." And Jesus said to him, "Truly, I say to you, this very night, before the cock crows twice, you will deny me three times."*

MARK 14:29-30

As a young man I used to think what a relief it would be to reach maturity and the older years. I was certain they would bring freedom from that constant battle with temptation. I looked at those older saints of God and envied the peace with God that must be theirs.

The passing years have taught me that Satan is no respecter of age. In fact he never lets up. He seems at times to act as though he is intensifying his efforts as life draws closer to the end. He seems to be trying to make the most of what time he has left.

As many other things crowd into our lives with the passing years, there is the growing temptation to neglect Bible study and private worship time. This throws one's life wide open for Satan to have free reign. He never neglects an open door! This is why Paul wrote, "Therefore let anyone who thinks that he stands take heed lest he fall" (I Corinthians 10:12). Paul was well along in life. He knew what he was talking about.

The only safeguard against sin at any age is a constant walk with God. There can be no letup. David once wrote, "I have walked in mine integrity; I have trusted also in the Lord; therefore I shall not slide" (Psalms 26:1 KJV). At that time he was walking close to God. He felt certain of his spiritual security. Later on, however, David was in a position of power, and was involved in many things. So somewhere along the way he let down his guard and left himself exposed to the devil's snares. Then he did things he never dreamed he would do. In great sorrow he wrote, "Have mercy upon me, O God, according to thy lovingkindness, according to the multitude of thy tender mercies, blot out my transgression" (Psalms 51:1 KJV).

Every day is a glorious opportunity to live for and serve God in Christ. But every day is also a day of danger. "Be sober, be watchful. Your adversary the devil prowls around like a roaring lion, seeking someone to devour. Resist him, firm in your faith, knowing that the same experience of suffering is required of your brotherhood throughout the world" (I Peter 5:8-9). Don't ever forget, you never cease to be his target to the very end of life!